America's Rural Yesterday

Volume IV: Early Tractors

Publisher of Rural Heritage Magazine

Publisher's Cataloging-in-Publication

America's rural yesterday. Volume IV, Early tractors /
featuring the photography of J.C. Allen & Son ; edited
by Joe Mischka.
pages cm
LCCN 2012953873
ISBN 9781882199020

1. Agriculture--United States--History--Pictorial
works. 2. Family farms--United States--History--
Pictorial works. 3. Country life--United States--
History--Pictorial works. I. Mischka, Joe,
editor. II. J. C. Allen & Son, photographer.
III. Title: Early tractors IV. Title: Early tractors.

S520.A44 2023 630'.973

Contents

Introduction

When we set out to publish a series of books featuring J.C. Allen & Son photos, we hadn't intended to include a book about early tractors. We tend to focus on draft animal farming and logging, so don't spend a lot of time covering tractors of any vintage.

However, a lot of our readers use mixed power on their farms. They include tractors and other power units as part of their strategy to get the job done. We don't subscribe to the notion that if a person farms with horses they ought not use tractors at all — as if they were breaking some kind of commandment. A lot of our friends use their horses, mules, oxen or donkeys when they can but will start up the tractor when the job calls for it. Much of the time, that tractor is an older model which handles the job just fine for them.

◦ ◦ ◦ ◦

I grew up on a hog farm where we had two Farmall tractors, a model C and an M. Actually, before the Farmalls — and before I was old enough to remember — we had an old John Deere model A my dad used for chores, picking corn with a one-row picker and other fieldwork. I don't remember the John Deere, but I have rich memories of the Farmalls. I watched my father and older brothers driving those tractors in the fields and the barnyard.

By the time I was old enough to drive a tractor — or, rather, by the time my older brothers had moved on to jobs off the farm — we had already transitioned from raising hogs to half-Arab saddle horses and then Percheron draft horses. In my teens, I drove horses as often as I drove a tractor on the farm. We used a team to clean the barn, ted and rake hay and handle other chores like cleaning the barn. But we still used the red tractors to cut and bale the hay, run a hay elevator off the PTO, and handle some of the heavier seedbed preparation.

To mow the hay, my dad would drive the smaller Farmall C tractor equipped with a 3-point hitch on which the mower hung, and I drove the bigger H tractor pulling an old crimper behind. A few years later, he bought a haybine which did both jobs at once, and I was no longer involved in hay cutting. I would use a team to ted the windrowed hay and then rake it with a side delivery rake.

We baled with the bigger tractor pulling a New Holland square baler. When I was little, my job was to walk along the baler and tug on the strings after the knotter engaged. If the twine pulled free, I would yell "whoa" as loud as I could so my dad could stop and we'd hand-tie that bale. I felt useful in that job.

We had two hay wagons, and, when one was stacked full, we used the small tractor to take it back to the barn. There we unloaded it using an old hay bale elevator running off a PTO-shaft off the old Farmall C. My older brothers were better at everything than I was. Peter was especially talented at stacking hay, both on the wagon as well as in the barn.

I loved those old tractors. They had their own personalities and seemed to be members of the farm crew, just like the teams we drove.

◦ ◦ ◦ ◦

The thing I like about tractors back in the day is they weren't too big. Many of the early tractors did about the same work as a good team of horses. In other words, they fit the scale of the farms back then. Today, of course, tractors and the implements they pull are giant machines that dwarf the men and women using them.

Our old tractors fit our 120-acre farm perfectly.

◦ ◦ ◦ ◦

This is a picture book with captions. For the most part, the captions do a good job of identifying the tractor models and attached implements. To come up with the names and models, I relied mostly on the help of David Brink of Bronson, Iowa, who has an almost ecyclopedic knowledge of old tractors as well as a collection of reference books he used to confirm his suppositions. Together we wrote the captions and later asked Sam "Let's Talk Rusty Iron" Moore, to proof our text. Both men were invaluable in putting this book together.

The J. C. Allen photo collection is an American treasure. It documents perfectly how things were done back in the day, who was doing it and with what tools. It is a treat to look through a stack of photos to choose which ones to use and come up with a caption. There are many thousands of images. Thankfully, J.C. Allen's son, John Allen, has the collection well organized and is able to put his hands on whatever I ask for. Many times, Allen wrote on the back of the print certain pertinent information such as the name and location of the farm, the operator and other details. But many times, the back of the print is blank.

° ° ° °

This is not a history book. We don't delve into the many interesting personalities involved in the evolution of the tractor or which company was bought out by which competitor. There are lots of books out there doing that well already. Along those same lines, it is not meant to be an exhaustive, all-encompassing look at the companies making the early tractors. We don't include every model or iteration.

Instead, we bring you, the reader, some of the best photos taken in the first half of the 20th Century of farmers using tractors in their farm fields and barnyards. Because Allen took photos for dealers and tractor companies to use in their advertisements, the photos are often of new, impeccably presented machines being used by the farm families who bought them.

— Joe Mischka

Imagine what it must have been like to walk into a showroom and see these machines new.

Chapter 1
Getting Started

The Indiana tractor developed by Star Tractor Company, Findlay, Ohio, is a front-end-drive tractor with a special hitch to which an implement — in this case, a corn binder — could be attached. Circa 1920.

An International Harvester Mogul 8-16 pulling a tandem set of discs weighted with logs and rocks in 1916. The stack on top of the tractor is expelling steam from the water cooling system.

An early Bates Steel Mule tractor on a Moline binder. This tractor has wheels in front, but a crawler track on the rear. The operator is running the tractor from the seat of the binder.

A farmer drills oats into corn stubble on an Avery model C motor-cultivator pulling a Van Brunt grain drill.

A 10-20 Mogul tractor pulls two right-hand grain binders that delivered the grain on the left side in 1919.

Above: An Avery tractor in 1918 pulls two modified horse drawn disc harrows. One set sports smooth blades while the other has notched discs. The front attachment provides self-steering with a wheel that rides in the furrow during plowing. A wooly sheepskin provides extra cusion for the driver.

Above right: A Titan 10-20 tractor and McCormic-Deering one-row corn picker on an Indiana farm.

Right: An Avery tractor pulls a heavy-duty wagon with an unidentified cargo and followed by a general use farm wagon.

This Avery tractor is pulling a horse drawn tandem disk with both smooth and notched blades The tractor wheels have been fitted with width extensions to provide more flotation.

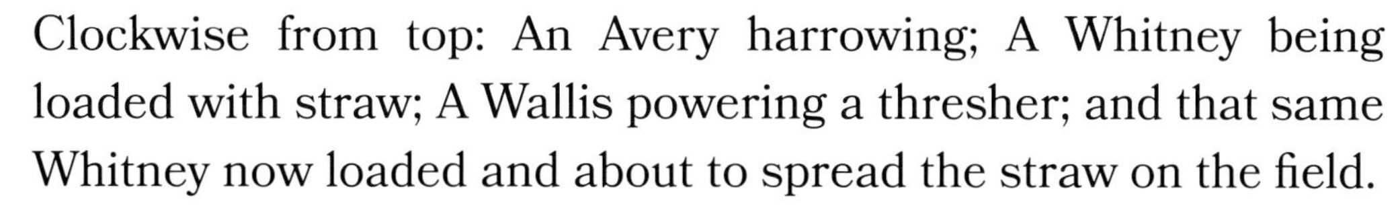

Clockwise from top: An Avery harrowing; A Whitney being loaded with straw; A Wallis powering a thresher; and that same Whitney now loaded and about to spread the straw on the field.

Chapter 2
Hart-Parr, Cletrac & Oliver

Baling clover hay on the farm of H.H. Hyland in Marshall, Mo., using a Hart-Parr tractor to power the hay press and a team of mules on a buck rake to bring in the hay.

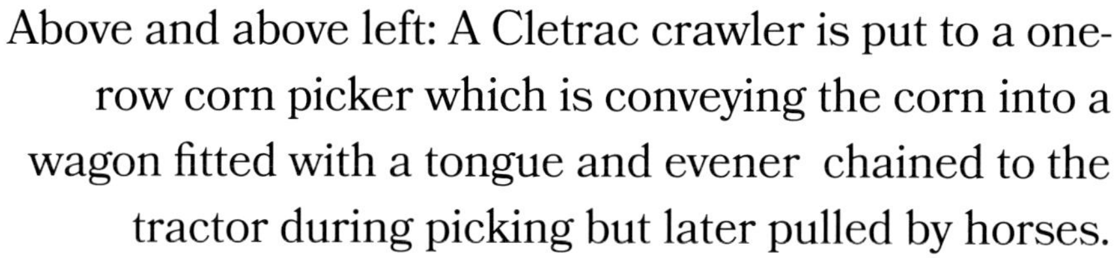
Above and above left: A Cletrac crawler is put to a one-row corn picker which is conveying the corn into a wagon fitted with a tongue and evener chained to the tractor during picking but later pulled by horses.

Right: The same model Cletrac crawler is being used to power a feed grinder on the farm of George Todd of Delphi, Ind. 1937.

Harvesting potatoes with a Cletrac crawler in 1940. Hundreds of bagged potatoes are in the background.

Ed Johnson of Paxton, Ill., cultivates checked corn with his Oliver Hart-Parr 70 Row-Crop tractor.

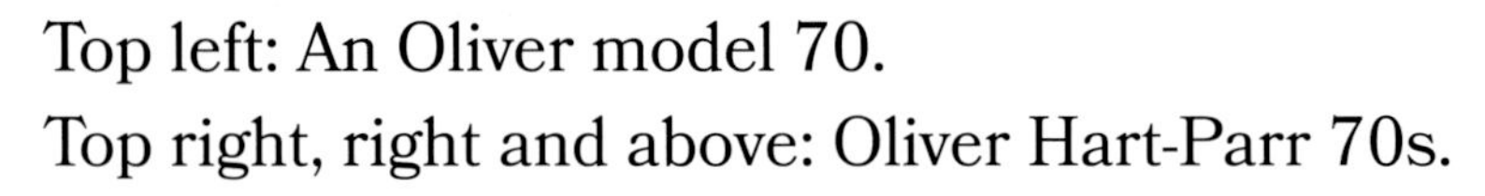

Top left: An Oliver model 70.

Top right, right and above: Oliver Hart-Parr 70s.

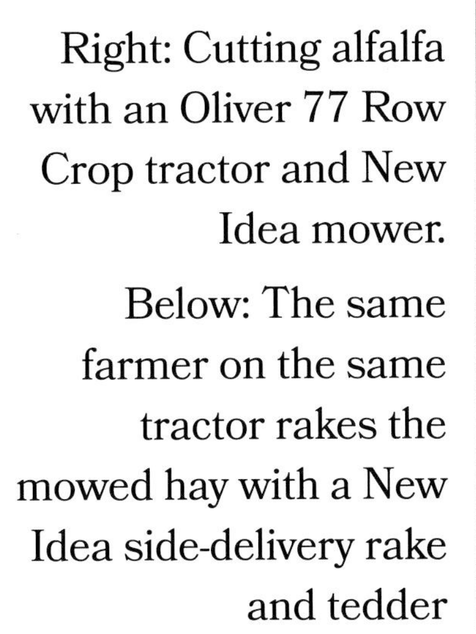

Right: Cutting alfalfa with an Oliver 77 Row Crop tractor and New Idea mower.

Below: The same farmer on the same tractor rakes the mowed hay with a New Idea side-delivery rake and tedder

OLIVER
60

OLIVER

Opposite Page: Cultivating corn with an Oliver Row Crop 60 tractor.
Above: An Oliver 70 Row-Crop with the cultivator shovels raised and pulling an aggressively-set spike-tooth harrow. The tractor rear wheels are weighted with concrete.

Left: An Oliver Row Crop 70 with steel wheels pulls a Soilfitter brand rotary hoe.
Above: An Oliver 70 Row Crop pulls a combine harvesting what appears to be clover. A large haystack is seen in the distance.

Right: An Oliver 50 road grader is put to use by the Ohio Engineering Company of Lorain, Ohio.

Below: An Oliver 99 industrial tractor pulls a sheepsfoot roller on the same project.

Chapter 3
Ford & Fordson

A hay or bundle rack, built with a platform on rails that can be moved from the back to the front, is hooked to an early Fordson tractor with its horsedrawn pole.

Left: A Fordson tractor is braced with a jack to maintain tension on the belt. .

Above: This photo was taken to illustrate the arrival of electric lights on the farm as a father and son work on their Fordson tractor.

A family shows off its Ford farm equipment as well as a big team of mules. The mother and three children sit in the Model T Ford automobile; a son sits on a Fordson tractor; and a young woman sits in the Ford truck. 1924.

A Fordson tractor pulls a grain binder in 1926.

A Fordson Tractor pulling tandem discs. 1928.

A Ford tractor cultivating what appears to be tomato plants in very dry ground. .

Above: A Ford tractor on a grain binder.

Opposite: A Ford 9N tractor on a disc harrow.

Above: A Ford tractor on a pasture cultivator on the Charles Parlan farm near Lafayette, Ind.

Above: Spraying herbicide on a corn crop with a Ford tractor.

A Ford tractor pulling a small load of cabbage.

A Ford tractor planting checked corn.

Chapter 4
Allis-Chalmers

Opposite Page: Drilling oats with double drills to an Allis-Chalmers UC tractor on the farm of Paul Boes, Tippecanoe County, Ind.

Above and Right: Diedrich Ubbinger of Tippecanoe County used his Allis-Chalmers tractor on a disc.

Using an Allis-Chalmers tractor pulling a disc and harrow to cover oats seed being broadcast in the background. The man in the wagon loads the hopper as the team walks ahead. On the farm of Everett Adwell near Otterbein, Ind. 1932.

The same turnout as on the previous page, this time driving away from the camera.

Top left: An Allis-Chalmers UC tractor on a cultipacker.

Above: New Allis-Chalmers model UC tractor pulling an Avery one-way Wheatland plow on the farm of John Sears in Lubbock, Texas.

Left: A UC tractor pulling two rotary hoes.

Above: Cultivating young corn on the farm of Gaines Beech, near Decatur, Ill., with an Allis-Chalmers UC tractor.

Top right and right: R.C. Low of Greenfield, Ind., plants corn with his Allis-Chalmers UC tractor pulling a converted horse drawn two row planter. 1935.

Above: Combining wheat on the Fall Circle Ranch owned by Frank Corn, Crosbyton, Texas, with an Allis-Chalmers UC tractor and Rumley combine.

Left: Discing and harrowing on the farm of E.C. Hagerty, Brookston, Ind., with an Allis-Chalmers model UC tractor.

An Allis-Chalmers model E 20-35 tractor powers an Allis-Chalmers clover huller. 1932.

Top left: William Wolf of Montmorenci, Ind., pulling a four bottom plow with an Allis-Chalmers model E 20-35 tractor.

Above: An Allis-Chalmers UC tractor working in maize pulling a lister cultivator outfit on the farm of F.L. Scott in Martin, Texas.

Left: Summer cultivation of a fallow field on the Ellsworth Sherman farm in Garden City, Kan., with Allis-Chalmers E 20-35 tractors pulling disc tillers.

An Allis-Chalmers model U tractor pulls an Allis-Chalmers combine. A team of horses on a dump rake can be seen in the background.

Top left: An Allis-Chalmers U tractor with an Allis-Chalmers combine.

Above: Plowing with an Allis-Chalmers model U tractor.

Left: Discing and harrowing oats with a 2-year-old Allis-Chalmers U belonging to William Wettschurack near Otterbein, Ind.

Greg Sanner of Bethany, Ill., pulls a rotary hoe with his Allis-Chalmers U tractor.

An Allis-Chalmers B tractor is put to a manure spreader being loaded with straw.

This Allis-Chalmers B tractor is fitted with dual wheels, both of which appear to be in the furrow.

Left: An Allis-Chalmers model M tractor pulls two wagons loaded with sugar cane near Canal Point, Fla., 1937.

Left: An Allis-Chalmers model KO pulls a "tractor train" of sugar cane from the field to the railroad in Canal Point, Fla.

An Allis-Chalmers M model pulls a disc harrow.

An Allis-Chalmers WC plants corn with a two-row corn planter mounted beneath.

An Allis-Chalmers WC model pulls a loaded manure spreader.

Above: An Allis-Chalmers WC pulls a two-bottom plow.
Left: An Allis-Chalmers WC cultivates corn on the Jesse McCain farm near Camden, Ind.

An Allis-Chalmers WC pulls up a fence post, using an iron wheel to provide upward leverage.

A young man plows with an Allis-Chalmers WC tractor.

Ralph Freshour of Medaryville, Ind., earns some extra money off the farm with his Allis-Chalmers WC tractor working on a new township road near his farm.

Straw is baled with a hay press powered by an Allis-Chalmers WC tractor.

An Allis-Chalmers WC and Number 3 combine at work on a farm near Lafayette, Ind.

Combining heavy rye with an Allis-Chalmers High Speed combine and Allis-Chalmers WC tractor owned and operated by Wendell Woodmansee of Marion, Ind.

An Allis-Chalmers WC model pulls a tandem disc.

An Allis-Chalmers WC cuts wheat with a binder in 1939.

Top: An Allis-Chalmers K model removes topsoil with a scoop in a limestone quarry so the site can be blasted to remove stone.

Left: Allis-Chalmers K and L models build a road near Vernon, Ind. The K operates a heavy grader while the L is put to four 2-yard scoops.

Above and top right: An Allis-Chalmers Speed Patrol road grader works in LaPorte County, Ind.

Right: An Allis-Chalmers model M pulls a large tandem disc harrow.

A hoist lifts the front of a wagon to unload the sweet corn hauled by the Allis-Chalmers tractor on the left.

Right: two Allis-Chalmers WC tractors work to prepare seedbed and plant seed.

Far right: An Allis-Chalmers WC tractor pulls a John Deere manure spreader.

An Allis-Chalmers WC tractor powers a feed grinder on the Bauder Bros. farm near North Liberty, Ind.

Chapter 5
Twin City & Minneapolis-Moline

One of the first gas-driven farm implements in Indiana, a Moline Universal tractor pulls a cultivator.

A Twin City 20-35 on a Russell Road Finisher grader. The 20-35 was introduced in 1920 and discontinued in 1927.

A Twin City 21-32 tractor pulling a four-bottom plow and spike tooth harrow at the Warren North farm in Brookston,

Left: A Moline Universal model D preparing a seedbed with a harrow and cultipacker in 1918.

Below: A Twin City MTA tractor with steel wheels pulling a plow and harrow in 1936.

A Twin City MTA is put to work at the 1935 National Corn Husking Contest held in Newtown, Ind.

Above: Jay Max of Oxford, Ind., uses a Twin City MTA tractor on an eight-blade disk tiller.
Left: Feeding beef cattle with a Twin City MTA tractor.

A Twin City MTA tractor on a grain binder.

A Twin City MTA tractor powers a threshing machine in 1939.

Top photos: cultivating corn with new Twin City MTAs. Above: plowing with a Twin City MTA on rubber tires, in Creston, Ind., in 1939. Left: Plowing with a new Twin City MTA tractor.

Cultivating young corn with a Twin City MTA tractor on rubber tires in 1935.

A Minneapolis-Moline RTU tractor on a two-row corn picker in 1941. The turck is an International model K-5.

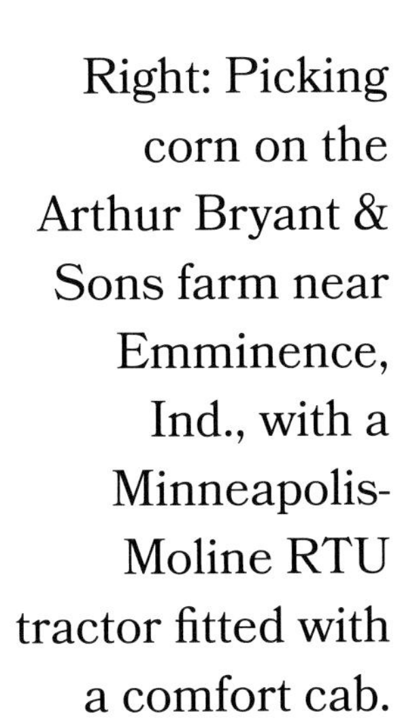

Right: Picking corn on the Arthur Bryant & Sons farm near Emminence, Ind., with a Minneapolis-Moline RTU tractor fitted with a comfort cab.

Left: A pair of Minneapolis-Moline RTU tractors harvest grain with two M-M combines. The tractor in the rear is fitted with an expansive sun shade.

Cultivating sugar beets near Hudsonville, Mich., with a Minneapolis-Moline model R tractor. 1941.

Left and below: Loading mixed hay on the Marshall Herbert farm in Delton, Mich., using a new Minneapolis-Moline hay loader and Minneapolis-Moline model R tractor.

Above: A Minneapolis-Moline KTA tractor is pulling a disk harrow followed by a drag. In the photo on the opposite page he has dropped the drag. 1936.

Right: A new Minneapolis-Moline KTA model tractor and three-bottom plow work on the farm of Ansel E. Rater of Lafayette, Ind. 1936.

Below: A Minneapolis-Moline KTA model tractor hauling sweet corn to the California Packing Company factory in Rochelle, Ill.

Left: A Minneapolis-Moline model JT tractor pulls a Minneapolis-Moline combine.

Below: A Minneapolis-Moline model JT tractor pulls a four-section Minneapolis-Moline harrow in Brookston, Ind.

A Minneapolis-Moline model JT tractor plows some wet ground.

Top left: Purney Myers, of Brookston, Ind., plowing with a Minneapolis-Moline JT.

Top right: Cultivating corn with a Minneapolis-Moline model JT tractor owned by Schertz Brothers of Gibson City, Ill.

Right: Discing with a M-M model JT tractor in Linden, Ind. 1937.

Above: A M-M model JT tractor culttivating.

A Minneapolis-Moline model UTU tractor aggressively hilling corn with a cultivator to improve irrigation between rows.

Left: A Minneapolis-Moline model UTU tractor picking corn. 1941.

Below: A Minneapolis-Moline model UTU tractor pulling a Minneapolis-Moline combine bagger.

A propane-burning Minneapolis-Moline model UTU tractor pulls a five-bottom plow. Hogs and piglets forage ahead. 1949.

Left: A Minneapolis-Moline model UTU tractor pulls a Minneapolis-Moline combine. 1940.

Below: A Minneapolis-Moline model UTU tractor is equipped with a front-mount cultivator.

Below left: A Minneapolis-Moline UTU pulls a Minneapolis-Moline side-delivery rake.

A Minneapolis Moline model ZTU tractor plowing in 1936.

Left. Mowing hay with a Minneapolis-Moline model ZTU tractor.

Below: A Minneapolis-Moline model ZTU tractor bales hay with a Case hay baler. Two men are mostly hidden near the discharge chute where they tie the bales.

Left. A Minneapolis-Moline model ZTU tractor is put to a four-row corn planter. 1938.

Below and opposite page: A Minneapolis-Moline model KT tractor operates a Minneapolis-Moline combine.

M·M

A Minneapolis-Moline model GB tractor pulling a vertical mulcher cutting grass and burying it in a trench.

Top Left: A Minneapolis-Moline ZTU cultivating corn.

Top Right: A Minneapolis-Moline ZTU pulling a Harvester Junior.

Above Right: A fenderless Minneapolis-Moline RTU harvesting wheat with a Harvester 69.

Above: A Minneapolis-Moline ZTU tractor plowing.

Chapter 6
International Harvester

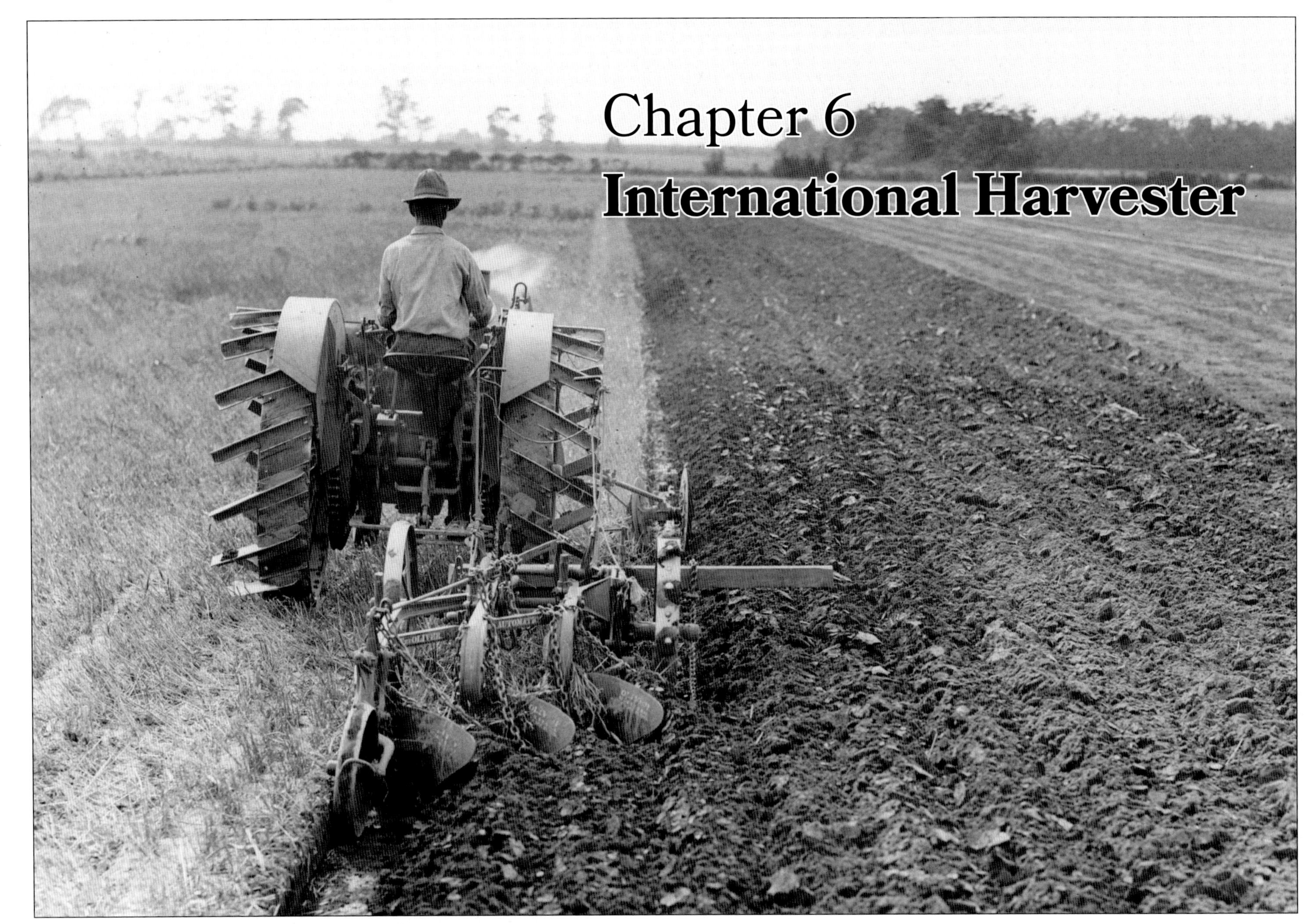

A Mogul 10-20 on a three-bottom Oliver plow. 1918.

A 10-20 Mogul tractor harvesting oats with binders delivering their bundles on the left side.

A Titan 10-20 threshing at the Lon McCoy farm in Decatur County, Ind.

Top left: Harvesting soybeans with a McCormick-Deering combine on farm of Charles Meharry near Odell, Ind. 1926.
Top right: Harvesting wheat with a combine on one of the farms of Purdue University near West Lafayette, Ind. Judging by the shocks of grain in the background, they opened up the field with a binder first.
Right and above: Cutting alfalfa with Farmall Regular model in Monroe, Iowa. The mower is mounted on the drawbar lowered for the implement.

Right and below: Cutting soybeans with a binder drawn by a Farmall Regular tractor and followed by a wheat drill pulled by four horses on the farm of Russell Butler and his father-in-law, William Dowson, near Lafayette, Ind. Mrs. Butler is driving the tractor.

Left: Archie Haxton pours wheat into a grain drill pulled by a McCormick-Deering 10-20 on the farm of Griff Quirk of Wingate, Ind.

Below: Archie pours fertilizer into the drill.

Hulling clover seed with A McCormick-Deering 10-20 tractor and Wood Bros. thresher at the farm of J. Berlowitz, Tippecanoe County, Ind.

Top: Preparing seed bed on the Henry W. Marshall farm, Tippecanoe County, Ind., with a 15-30 McCormick Deering tractor pulling a set of discs and double-roller.
Above left and above right: Drilling wheat on the farm of Finis Fouts, Deer Creek, Ind. The drill is operated by a Farmall tractor and preceded by a disc.

Farmall Regular tractor with a mounted McCormick-Deering No. 20 Corn picker at work on the farm of Gov. Warren T. McCray, Kentland, Ind.

Top left: Loading an International truck with combined wheat on the Purdue University farm, West Lafayette, Ind. 1933.
Top right: A couple two-row model 112 McCormick-Deering corn planters joined with factory kit pulled by a Farmall Regular on the farm of ex-governor Warren T. McCray, Kentland, Ind.
Above right: Spreading lime with a wheat drill drawn by a Farmall Regular tractor on the farm of Homer Thrush, Wabash County, Ind. The drill operator, covered with lime, has tied his pants legs to keep the fertilizer out.
Above left: Grading and sacking potatoes with homemade outfit pulled by a Farmall Regular with a generator and headlamp on the John Morsey farm near Antigo, Wis.

An early Farmall F-20 powers a Joseph Dick & Co. ensilage cutter that is blowing the chopped hay into a hay dryer powered by a McCormick-Deering P-20 or P-30 stationary power unit at Purdue University.

Top left: A Farmall F-30 tractor pulling a McCormick-Deering PTO-driven tractor grain binder.

Above: Harvesting sweet clover with a combine and McCormick-Deering tractor on the farm of Ernest Pierce, Swayzee, Ind.

Left: Hauling sweetcorn to the Illinois Canning factory Hooperton, Ill., using a new McCormick-Deering W-30 owned by Orville Storm, Hoopeston, Ill.

Top left: An IHC model H Baling Straw. Boone County, Ind. 1940.

Above: I.D. Meyer of the Purdue University Engineering Department devised this method of baling straw or hay by pulling a hay press attached to a hayloader, which feeds the hay into a chute, which, in turn, is fed into the baler. In this photo they are using an International model 15-30.

Left: An International model 8-16 tractor on a two-bottom Oliver plow.

Top left: A Titan 10-20 tractor pulls two grain binders.

Top right: A Farmall F-20 moves alfalfa with a buck rake.

Right: A Farmall F-20 with heavy cast wheels is repaired.

Above: Combining oats on Purdue University farm, West Lafayette, Ind., with a McCormick-Deering 15-30.

Chapter 7
J. I. Case

Threshing oats on the farm of Alfred Drake, Forreston, Ill., with a Case model L tractor and Case threshing machine.

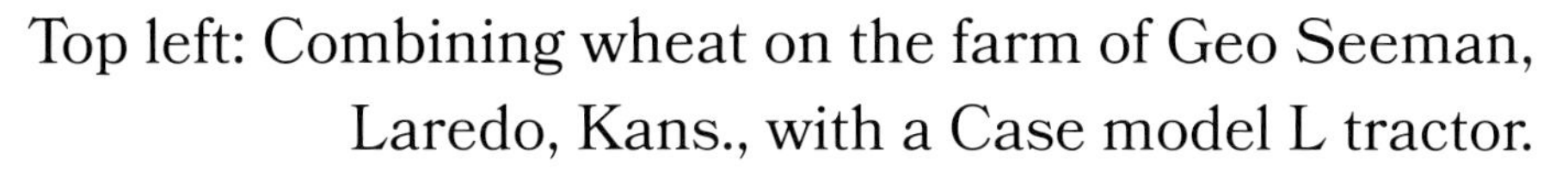

Top left: Combining wheat on the farm of Geo Seeman, Laredo, Kans., with a Case model L tractor.

Top right: Power pickup baler in alfalfa on farm of R.M. Jaimison, Garden City, Kans., pulled by a Case model CC tractor with a Case pull hay press.

Right: Planting corn and soybeans for forage on the *Breeders Gazette* farm near Spencer, Ind., with a Case model CC tractor.

Above: Using a disc tiller on the farm of Roy Mask, Clovis, N.M., with a Case CC tractor.

Top left: Laying out irrigation ditches with a Case CO in the young orange grove of Theodore Curtiss, Bryn Mawr, Calif.

Above: A model C Case pulling heavy model T truckload of rice from the ditch on farm of Henry Bull, Stuart, Ark.

Left: A Case-Industrial power unit runs a road maintainer in Delaware County, Ind. When the canvas under the roof is unrolled, it protects the power unit from the weather.

A model L Case tractor threshes rice in Devers, Texas.

Above: New Case CC preparing seed bed on the muck crop farm of Leo Balsey, Bremer, Ind.

Right: Threshing wheat with a new Case CC tractor and 22-inch Case separator owned by James Stephens and son, Frankfurt, Ind.

Opposite Page: Farmers look over a Case CC tractor and other equipment at a meeting hosted by the Case company.

CASE

A farmer operates a Case CC tractor by remote as he binds oats in 1938.

Above: A Case CC tractor pulls a Case combine harvesting soybeans.

Right: Threshing wheat with a new Case 28-47 separator and a Case model L tractor owned by Arthur Rusk, New Berlin, Ill.

Shoveling corn from a feed wagon pulled by a Case VAC tractor.

Above: Threshing barley with a Case 28-47 separator. and Case L tractor. Winchester, Ky. 1937.

Right: A Case DC powering a threshing machine

Two men feed bundles into a Case threshing machine being powered by a Case L model tractor.

Threshing with a Case 28-inch separator and a case CC model tractor. 1936.

Chapter 8
Caterpillar

Plowing with a Caterpillar model 10 in 1930.

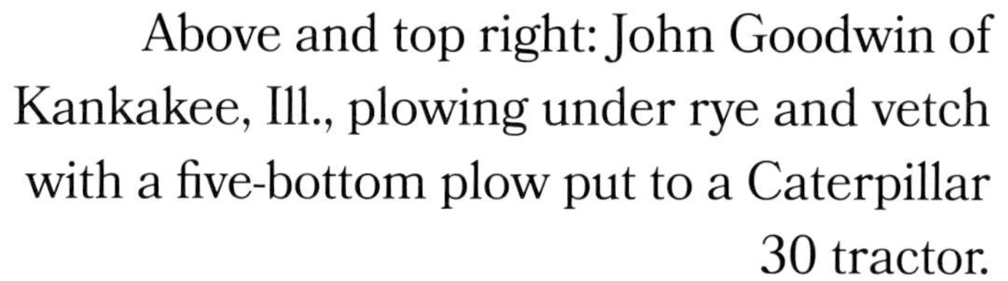

Above and top right: John Goodwin of Kankakee, Ill., plowing under rye and vetch with a five-bottom plow put to a Caterpillar 30 tractor.

Right: A Caterpillar 35 pulls a road grader on a dirt road near Tunica, Miss.

Caterpillar

CATERPILLAR

Opposite top: A Cat 22 plows some rough ground in 1935.

Opposite bottom: A Cat RD4 and a Minneapolis-Moline 28-inch separator threshing. 1936.

Above: A Cat R5 1937.

Top right: A Cat RD6 pulling out a large tree as part of a bypass construction project. 1936.

Right: Threshing oats with a Cat RD4 providing the power. 1940.

Chapter 9
John Deere

A John Deere model A tractor binding wheat with a power binder.

Above: Combining oats with a John Deere A in Gilliam, La., in 1943.

Above right and right: Plowing with a John Deere model A tractor and John Deere model 4B plow owned by A.C. Oilerand son, Brookston, Ind.

Picking corn with a John Deere model A tractor on a No. 25 mounted corn picker. The steering wheel below and to the left of the driver is used to engage the flywheel hidden by the corn picker to start the tractor.

Left and below: A John Deere model A pulls a four-section rotary hoe.

A John Deere model A tractor and No. 17 combine.

Above: A John Deere model A on a two-bottom plow.

Right: Cultivating young corn with a new Goodrich-equipped John Deere model A tractor owned by P. L. White of Oxford, Ind.

Above: New John Deere model A and model B tractors and a new combine are on display at the the New Ross, Ind., John Deere dealership. A flatcar with tractors is visible in the background on the right.

Right: A closeup of the flatcar loaded with John Deere tractors. The lugs for the steel wheels are in a pile at the end of the car.

Opposite top and bottom: A John Deere GP tractor powers a hay press baling straw. The press is mounted on rubber tires.

DEERE

An earlier model John Deere D is fitted with extension rims on the back wheels and pulls a John Deere model 5 combine.

A John Deere model D tractor powers a 28-inch thresher.

John Deere model GP tractor pulling and powering a John Deere tractor binder.

George Blain pulls a tandem disc weighted with bags of rocks behind a John Deere D tractor.

A John Deere model D tractor pulls a disc and spike tooth harrow on the farm of Dr. John S. Morrison of Lafayette, Ind., while a team of horses pulls a two-row corn planter.

A John Deere D tractor powers a John Deere thresher.

A John Deere model G tractor powers a 28-inch threshing machine blowing straw directly into the barn.

A John Deere model H is pulling a John Deere Van Brunt drill with a special attachment to plant soybeans in 28-inch rows.

Planting potatoes with a John Deere H tractor. The person on the two-row planter monitors the delivery system and raises and lowers the planters.

A John Deere model H tractor on a John Deere No. 55 four-row planter.

A John Deere model H tractor on a John Deere 290 two-row planter.

A John Deere model B tractor mows a roadside ditch with a John Deere model No. 5 mower.

Top left and above: A John Deere model B plowing with a two-bottom John Deere plow.

Left: A John Deere B tractor cutting oats with a PTO-driven tractor binder and driven by William Lehmann of Francesville, Ind.

Above: Robert Eckstein discs his family's field near Wooster, Ohio, with a John Deere model B tractor and tandem discs. The tractor is equipped with a lifter attachment to accept a John-Deere two-way plow.

Top left: Plowing under stubble with a John Deere B tractor

Above: A John Deere B tractor mowing flax with a model 5 mower with windrow attachment. 1939.

Left: A John Deere B tractor spreading manure with a John Deere model H manure spreader fitted with truck wheels.

Left: A John Deere B tractor pulling a John Deere one-bottom plow

Bottom Left: A John Deere model B tractor with two-row cultivator with power lift.

Below: A new model B tractor is driven out of the Brower Motor Company John Deere dealership in South Lafayette, Ind., in December 1944.

The Brower Motor Company was an authorized John Deere dealer in South Lafayette in 1944. During wartime, farmers were encouraged to maintain a rigorous maintenance schedule, as food production was a critical part of the war effort at home and equipment manufacturing had largely shifted from agricultural to military machinery, meaning fewer new tractors were available for purchase. A new model B tractor is pictured on the left, while two model A tractors are serviced.

A John Deere B tractor cultivates expertly check-planted corn rows.

Top left: A farmer uses a John Deere single disc behind a John Deere B tractor. He is going back over ground he worked in the other direction.

Above: The same farmer is using a four-section drag behind the same tractor.

Left: A John Deere B tractor moves a poultry house built on a sled.

Chapter 10
Massey-Harris

A Massey-Harris tractor pulls an Adams Road Maintainer grader in 1933.

Left: A Massey-Harris Super 101 tractor drills wheat in the early 1940s.

Below: A Massey-Harris Super 101 and No. 52 cultivator work a contoured field in 1940.

A Massey-Harris "Challenger" tractor plows under a weedy field.

A Massey-Harris 101 tractor pulls a Massey-Harris clipper combine in 1942.

Chapter 11
Silver King

A Silver King tractor put to a plow. 1936.

A Silver King picks corn with a New Idea corn picker. 1936.

Chapter 12
Heider

A team of Percherons pull a Heider tractor which appears to be experiencing some trouble in wet soil.

Cultivating with a Rock Island Heider 6-10 model M-2 motor cultivator. 1927.

Chapter 13
Huber

Arthur Cook cutting wheat with his combine for Frank Kerkoff, Montgomery, Ind., at $2.50 per acre. He uses a Massey-Harris combine and a Huber tractor.

Above: A Huber LC tractor pulls a two-bottom plow.

Right: John G. McKee of Lafayette, Ind., plowing with a Huber tractor and three bottom Oliver plow with harrow attachment.

1920 Indiana State Fair